Praise for Paul Ferrini's Books

"The most important book I have read. I study it like a bible!" Elisabeth Kubler-Ross, M.D.

"These words embody tolerance, universality, love and compassion—hallmarks of all Great Teachings. They turn our attention inward to our own divine nature, instead of diverting it outward. Paul Ferrini is a modern-day Kahlil Gibran—poet, mystic, visionary, teller of truth." Larry Dossey, M.D.

"Paul Ferrini leads us skillfully and courageously beyond shame, blame and attachment to our wounds into the depths of self-forgiveness. His work is a must-read for all people who are ready to take responsibility for their own healing." John Bradshaw.

"A breath of fresh air in an often musty and cluttered domain. With sweetness, clarity, and simplicity we are directed to the truth within. I read this book whenever my heart directs, which is often." Pat Rodegast.

"Paul Ferrini's writing is authentic, delightful and wise. It reconnects the reader to the Spirit Within, to that place where even our deepest wounds can be healed." Joan Borysenko, Ph.D.

"I feel that this work comes from a continuous friendship with the deepest part of the Self. I trust its wisdom." Coleman Barks, poet and translator.

"Paul Ferrini's wonderful books show a way to walk lightly with joy on planet earth." Gerald Jampolsky, M.D.

"Paul Ferrini leads us on a gentle journey to our true source of joy and happiness—inside ourselves." Ken Keyes, Jr.

Book Design by Paul Ferrini
Layout by Aryeh Swisa

ISBN # 1-879159-37-6

Manufactured in the United States of America

Grace Unfolding

&

The Art of Living
A Surrendered Life

PAUL FERRINI

Table of Contents

Introduction

Part One: The Surrendered Mind

Part Two: The Surrendered Heart

Part Three: The Surrendered Life

Part Four: Grace Unfolding

Introduction

⁂

What We Surrender

What We Surrender

In a worldly sense, surrender is not desirable. It is neither appropriate nor beneficial to give up one's power to another person, regardless of the position, lineage or symbolic value that person might have.

The kind of surrender we are talking about in this book is not a surrender to an outside authority, but to an inside one. When we talk about surrender here, we are talking about the surrender of our ego consciousness, our separated states of heart and mind, to a greater, more integral consciousness.

The assumption here is that each one of us is capable of tapping into that greater consciousness and living out from it, instead of living out from the fragmented consciousness of the wounded victim. Or to put it quite simply, we are capable of moving through our fears into the essence of love which is the Source of who we are.

Here we are surrendering to the truth of our

being. We are surrendering to an inner certainty, to the part of us that knows without knowing how it knows. Surrender means giving up our need to control our life, figure things out, or predict the future. It means letting go of our judgments and interpretations of life, indeed of everything that stands between us and our peace.

Much of who we think we are is a composite of our fears and the defensive mechanisms born of those fears. While these defenses may keep us safe, they also keep us frozen. In that state of contraction, we cannot realize our true Self or the true Self of others.

Our realization happens only in the present moment. To be here fully, we must be willing to let go of the past and meet the future with open arms. That often means letting the doors that brought us here close behind us.

Surrendering our past without knowing what the future will bring requires trust in ourselves, in others and in the nature of reality. When we can be fully present and aware in the midst of that apparent uncertainty, we are clearly guided to take the next step in our lives.

In truth, it is a step by step journey. We may have a sense of where we are going, but we don't know exactly how or when we are going to get there. At each juncture in our experience, the next step is revealed to us. That is the way that grace unfolds in our life.

Who Surrenders?

One who is fearful cannot surrender. The contracted, defensive, egoic states of consciousness cannot surrender. They cannot yield. They can only deepen in their judgment and subsequent fall from grace.

Beyond our judgment and our fear, there is one who understands and forgives, who holds everything that happens in our lives with great compassion. Knowing that S/he is loved and accepted, S/he can offer that unconditional love and acceptance to you.

S/he is the one who holds the wounded child,

calming and reminding it that it is safe. In her loving arms, the screams of the child diminish. Terror disappears and safety returns.

Remember, you are the child kicking and screaming and the one who holds that child with compassion. You are the one who judges and attacks and the one who forgives and atones for the attack. Lest you learn to hold your anger, your fear, your frustrated expectations with compassion, how can grace come into your life?

Part One

&

The Surrendered Mind

Mindstuff

The mind has so many thoughts. Some are uplifting. Some are depressing. Some are inspirational. Some are scary. At any moment, many different thoughts are going through our minds. If we take a deep breath and get quiet, we can witness this parade of thoughts.

Most of our thoughts appear and disappear on the screen of our minds. We don't pay very much attention to them.

But occasionally, we identify with a thought. Identification with a thought gives that thought power. It gives it attention. If the thought is a pleasant thought, it leads to other thoughts of pleasure. We daydream, fantasize, desire this or that.

If the thought is a negative thought, it leads to other distressing thoughts. We begin to build up a fearful picture.

When we give a lot of attention to a thought,

it often triggers an emotional reaction. When our feelings are stirred, it is not very easy to stay aware of the thoughts we are thinking. Instead, we become the reactive victim of those thoughts.

Judgment Layer

In addition to the thoughts we think, the mind also contains the judgments we have about the thoughts we are thinking. We like this thought, but not that one. This thought is spiritual; that thought isn't, and so forth.

Each of us has a running commentary on what we are thinking. We also have a running commentary on what anyone else might be verbalizing to us. We are always interpreting, analyzing, comparing this to that.

This judgment layer of mind can be very thick. We think something. Then we judge it. Then we judge our judgment of it, and so on. It can get fairly turgid and convoluted.

16

Clear Mind/Awareness

Beneath the judgment layer is the witness consciousness, the layer of Self that simply sees what is going on. It sees the thought and the judgment of the thought. It sees all the interpretations, all the ambivalent movement back and forth from one thought to another.

When we get quiet, we sink down to this level of pure awareness. We do not identify with our thoughts or our judgments. We just witness them.

Sometimes, right in the middle of our awareness, the witness goes to sleep, and we start identifying with our judgments. Then, the witness wakes up, and our simple awareness is restored.

The more we stay in witness consciousness, the more calm our minds are. Thoughts come and go, but we know that we are not those thoughts.

We begin to rest in something larger than thought, something that holds those thoughts compassionately. You can call it awareness. You can call it silence. It is the place from which thoughts spring, and to which they return. There, mind is clear, like the surface of a lake when there is no wind. There, mind is at peace.

Open Mind

Peace and clarity are the attributes of an open mind. An open mind is not identified with specific thoughts. It does not cherish opinions or harbor prejudices. It is not preoccupied with judgments, interpretations, or analysis.

An open mind can respond easily to the challenges of the moment. It is unfettered and free. It does not dwell on the past or think about the future. It is present right here and right now. As a result, it is open to all of the possibilities that arise.

The mind closes down when it identifies with its thoughts or judgments. Its focus narrows. It cannot see all the options that are available.

Making up Our Minds

When we make up our minds about something, we narrow our focus. We commit to a certain way of thinking.

A mind that is made up is not an open mind. It is a mind that is poised to act in a specific way, a mind that has limited its options.

However, not all action requires a narrowing of focus. Sometimes, we become aware that a specific action is needed and we take it. We don't deliberate. Nor do we feel regret.

When the action is complete, we return to openness. We see where we are and what is possible now. Just because we acted in a certain way does not mean that we need to continue to act in that way.

The mind opens and closes. We identify with something and then return to simple awareness. We don't let ourselves get stuck in a rigid, untenable position.

A flexible mind opens and closes. It never stays shut. It constantly reconsiders its position as new information comes its way.

Dogmatic thinking closes the mind. Rigid belief systems confine the mind in a prison of its own making.

When fear comes up, we all have a tendency to want to put everything into a box and tie it up. But boxes are meant to be opened.

Life doesn't fit into precise containers. It overflows the banks, outgrows the form through which it expresses.

Mind expands and contracts. It narrows and widens its focus. That flexibility is the key to living a life that is responsive and free.

Changing Our Minds

When we don't make our minds up prematurely or rigidly hold onto the positions we take, we don't have to change our minds very often. We may modify our position, but we don't need to flip flop.

When we make mistakes, we can acknowledge them and set a new course of action. Mistakes usually arise when we act before we are clear, or when we are attached to an old position that needs to shift.

When we are not attached to an old position or

moving impulsively toward a new one, we can choose the best course of action in the moment. The next moment may require a different action, but we won't know it until we get there.

Life is dynamic. It is constantly changing. The awareness we have right now may not be the awareness we have tomorrow or next week.

Steadfast in our actions, we can allow for change. Flexible in our thinking, we can be ready to commit when the time is right.

Conflict and Ambivalence

There are times when we go back and forth between one thought and its opposite. We become attached to both positions at the same time. We want our security and we want our freedom. However, they seem to be at odds. Our perception is dualistic.

To act out of conflict or ambivalence is asking for trouble. This is not a time to act, but to be present and acknowledge our attachment to both ends of the spectrum. It is a time to sink down through our thoughts and judgments into witness consciousness.

When we do that, we take the pressure off. We don't have to decide before we are ready. We wait. We watch. And sooner or later something shifts, in our own perception perhaps, and/or in the outside situation.

We should never make decisions when we are conflicted or ambivalent. If we do, those decisions are likely to cause suffering for ourselves and others.

This is the best time to get quiet and listen. It is the best time to meditate, go on retreat, hike in the woods, or go fishing. Doing something concrete and physical which gets us out of our heads is the best way to allow mental conflict to subside.

Resting in the Storm

Whenever we are feeling tense or pressured, it's time to back off. These are signs that a storm is brewing in the mind.

Let's take a deep breath and go out for a walk. Let's get present in our bodies.

Now is not the time to decide. It is time to take the pressure off.

We acknowledge that we have contradictory thoughts. We admit that we don't know what to think or what to do.

We breathe and let life be just the way it is. We stop trying to make things happen. We accept things as they are.

We rest in the storm and let the storm pass over us. Storms do not last forever.

We surrender the problem. We surrender our need to surrender the problem. We let everything be okay the way it is.

We accept the unfinishedness of life in this moment. We know the package is not wrapped neatly. It can't be helped. The tape and scissors are nowhere to be found.

It will be easier to deal with wrapping the package at a different time.

The storm comes and goes. The rains pelt us and the winds blow us. That is just the way it is. It's not our fault.

Storms may arise in consciousness, but consciousness is more than the storm. It is also the sky in which the storm appears.

Behind the clouds is blue sky and sun. When the rain comes down, we remember this. When great gusts of wind drive us to seek shelter, we remember the calm before the storm.

Like a tree, we endure this weather, our branches shaking in the wind, remembering that in time the clouds will part and the sun will come out to dry our leaves.

Mind contains storm, tree and sky. It is the one who acts, the one who is acted upon, and the one who observes the action.

You are all of this and more. Inside you dwells the cause of your pain and your freedom from suffering.

Part Two

❧

The Surrendered Heart

Heartstuff

Our hearts are filled with desires. Some of them are contradictory. We want to share our lives with another person and we want our autonomy. We want a more interesting, creative job and we want the security our present job provides.

When we are ambivalent about what we want, we bring that desire into our lives in an ambivalent way. When we are clear about what we want and committed to it, we bring the desired outcome in with integrity.

Often, we need to experience something we think we want in a negative way. Then we know it's not what we really want. That helps us move out of ambivalence.

We don't have to beat ourselves up for this. It is the way that we learn. Sometimes we have to say no to one thing, before we can say yes to something else.

Fears

Our desires tend to be conflicted because we are attached to the way things are. Even if we don't like the way things are and desire something different, we are afraid to let go of what is familiar. What is known is comforting to us, even when we don't like it. We know how to handle it. We don't know how to handle the unknown. What is unfamiliar is always scary to us.

It is not surprising then that we frequently find ourselves in the position of being afraid of what we desire. Needless to say, this incapacitates us. We keep swinging back and forth between the extremes of wanting and not wanting. It is emotionally draining to ourselves and others when we vacillate back and forth between saying yes and saying no. All we can do to find peace in this situation is to be aware of both our desire and our fear and rest in that awareness.

As we do so, we sink down through our fear and our desire into something which is greater than both. That is our simple acceptance of ourselves right now in the midst of conflict or ambivalence. We may be struggling by wanting something we are afraid of, but we can accept without reservation the person who is struggling. When we do that, desire and fear rest together in a more peaceful place, and integration happens.

We don't repress our desires, nor do we indulge them. We don't rush ahead blindly or retreat in fear. We move forward slowly. We find a middle ground, a way to be honest with every-thing we are feeling. We learn to tell ourselves the truth. And that makes it possible for us to tell others the truth too.

When we accept all of our feelings, we can be authentic. We don't have to pretend to be someone or something we are not. We don't need to be deceptive with others or to feel guilty for lying to them or misleading them.

Telling the truth to ourselves and others helps to neutralize any harm that can result from our ambivalence. The truth gives us the freedom to be ourselves, to experience our conflict instead of stuffing it, and to attend to our own need for healing.

Finding out What we Really Want

Generally, when we acknowledge our fears — when we bring them into our conscious focus — we begin to move through them. Once our fears have gotten our attention, they don't run us any more. Instead, we move through them consciously, step by step, in full awareness. This creates integration and congruence in our psyche.

But sometimes our fears are very strong. They remain a troublesome presence, even when we acknowledge them. When our fears come into our conscious attention and they don't diminish, we need to realize that we may not be ready for the action we say we want to take. We may need to admit to ourselves and others "I'd like to do this, but I can see I'm not ready yet."

Sometimes it doesn't feel safe to take a particular risk. So, we can't take it in good faith. If we do take it, we might be setting ourselves and others up for disappointment. In this case, it is better to wait until we feel ready.

It may take us a while to move through certain fears. We can't rush the process. It will take as long as it takes. We will know when we are ready.

Often people want us to do things we are not ready to do. In the attempt to please them, we violate ourselves. Then, when all is said and done, everyone feels hurt. This pattern can be broken if we will acknowledge the depth of our fears, first to ourselves and then to others.

Fear is not necessarily a bad thing. It simply asks us to pay attention to something. Once we start paying attention, the fear dissolves. It has served its purpose.

Sometimes, we need to pay attention for a day or so. Sometimes, we need to pay attention for several years. Not all fears require the same amount of attention.

Once we have listened to the fear, it should diminish. If it doesn't, we need to keep paying attention. That might mean being consciously aware of our fear, or it might mean backing away from an action that secretly terrifies us.

When we allow the fear to come into our awareness, we will get in touch with a part of ourselves we may be neglecting or tuning out. Listening to that part of ourselves will help us think and act in a way that addresses our whole reality.

Fear only runs our lives when it is unconscious. Then, it can undermine our goals and prevent us from taking risks we are ready to take.

When we acknowledge our fear, we can integrate it into our total psychic awareness. Then, it will not be able to hold us back from taking actions which our soul needs to grow. However, it may help us slow down and avoid impulsive actions that do not serve us.

Our awareness begins to break down chronic fears that are ready to dissolve. It also highlights fears we may be repressing so that we can come to grips with them. Being aware of our fears creates balance in our psyche. It helps to slow us down when it's time to slow down. And it helps to give us a boot in the pants when it's time to start moving.

It is ironic, but sometimes we can feel scared about taking a risk and at the same time know that we are safe taking it. That is the way it is with most fears.

But sometimes we feel scared and don't know that we are safe. When that happens, we need to take a good look at our life. We may not be ready to proceed with our plans. We may need to take a step backwards, or retreat completely.

This dialog with our fear is an essential aspect of creating unity and integration in our psyche. We are never going to make our fear go away. The attempt to do so just gives that fear subconscious power over us. Instead, we need to invite it in, listen to it, dialog with it, and then make emotionally informed decisions.

Creating Emotional Balance

Lack of balance occurs when we allow our fears to prevent us from taking risks that are essential to our growth. Lack of balance also occurs when we ignore our fears and insist on taking risks we are not emotionally ready to take. In the first case, we cut ourselves off artificially from others. In the second case, we make commitments to others we can't possibly keep. Both extremes result in emotional pain and isolation.

If we have one of these extremes operating in our lives, we need to take note of it and begin to move toward the center. People who ignore or override their fears and act before they are emotionally ready need to slow down, listen to their fears, and wait until they are ready to act. People who hold onto their fears and use them as an excuse for not expressing themselves creatively need to practice taking small risks that can open up new possibilities in their lives.

Every person needs a balance between challenge and safety. The former is the masculine, creative energy of the universe. It brings in change and is an awakening force. The latter is the feminine, receptive energy of the universe. It brings stability and is a nurturing force.

Each one of us needs both masculine and feminine energies. We need challenge and safety, change and stability, awakening and nurturing. The more balanced we are in this respect the better. Then, we don't have to rely on our relationships as the only means for creating psychic balance in our lives.

Trust

When we have been hurt, we stop trusting others. Our hearts shut down. We are no longer emotionally available to ourselves or others.

Many of us have trust issues because we have trusted inappropriate people in the past. We then use this as an excuse for not trusting others, who may be worthy of our trust.

When we trust people who are not trustworthy, it usually suggests that we don't trust ourselves. When we trust ourselves, we are not drawn to untrustworthy people.

We attract to us people who mirror back to us

how we feel about ourselves. If trust is our issue, we need to own it, instead of trying to make it someone else's responsibility.

Trusting ourselves means that we acknowledge our fears about others and take the time to get to know them. We don't sleep with people we don't know. We don't become emotionally involved with strangers. We take the time to find out who others are and how we feel being with them. Then, if we feel comfortable with someone, we open up gradually.

The heart does not need to be pried open. It opens naturally if we give it time.

If we are feeling insecure and unlovable, we may rush into relationships before really checking out our potential partners. We pay for our impulsiveness by getting hurt and shutting down. We think it was the other person who was not trustworthy. But in truth, we were not trustworthy. We jumped into something before we knew we were really comfortable. We acted impulsively and irresponsibly.

Maybe the other person did the same. So we are both responsible. The problem of trust doesn't just belong to the other person. It belongs to us too. We have not learned to trust ourselves. That's why we choose to get involved with people who aren't trustworthy.

An Open Heart

Those who take the time to get to know each other don't trust each other prematurely. Each trusts the other as that person shows that s/he is trustworthy. It is a process.

It is an error to think that an open heart is a foolish one. An open heart says "I'm willing to trust you as long as it feels that we are opening to each other. If this changes, I will be more cautious."

To be "cautious" does not mean to shut down. It means to go slowly, to keep our eyes open, to keep checking in with ourselves and the other person day by day.

Nothing closes a heart more prematurely than diving into a relationship without knowing who the other person is. That is not a sign of trust for the other person. That is a complete disregard for the necessity of building mutual trust before such an action is taken.

Trust should not be blind. It must be cultivated over time. Then it becomes conscious and reliable.

When trust is progressive in this manner, each person gradually reveals himself. There is a deepening of knowledge and sympathy. This prepares the space into which love can be born.

In spite of beliefs to the contrary, it is not necessary to cut off our heads to dwell in our hearts. Head and heart need to learn to work together. It is in their mutual intercourse that the seeds of integration and equality are sewn.

Synergy of Head and Heart

When we realize that we have a pattern of disregarding our fears/desires or being run by them, we need to step back and look at the pattern. The mind helps us to do this. It helps us see the big picture.

We see how our insecurity and emotional neediness lead to impulsive actions that get us involved in inappropriate relationships. Or we see how our fears prevent us from opening our hearts to the possibility of new, healthy relationships. We understand our pattern so that we can see it the next time it manifests in our lives. Then we can make conscious choices, instead of unconscious ones.

This doesn't mean that we analyze our lives to death. We don't escape into our heads. We learn to detach emotionally just enough to gain perspective on our situation. The mind understands what the heart feels. The heart listens to what the mind sees. They commune. And, as they do, integration happens in the psyche.

We want to make choices that honor what we feel and are consistent with the goals that we have set for our lives. Heart and head need to be in constant dialog if we are to make sensitive, intelligent choices.

Sometimes we act based on a feeling that

something is right, even though the mind is skeptical. We need to pay attention to the outcome when we act intuitively. Do we make good choices when we do this? If we do, we want to keep trusting our intuition. If we don't, we need to question whether it is really intuition we are following. Sometimes what we call intuition is just our desire or our fear run amuck.

As we experiment, we get to know our strengths and weaknesses. We learn to ascertain when we are ambivalent and when we are clear, when we are open and intuitive and when we are emotionally reactive. We get to know our emotional landscape. That is important work. We can't live in our hearts if we are unwilling to undertake this exploration.

Surrendering to the Truth of our Being

As we become aware of our desire and fear and learn to hold them compassionately, we sink down to a place in our hearts of perfect peace.

There, we know that we are safe regardless of how many fears come up. We know we are worthy, even though we have wants or needs that aren't being met. There, we can accept our lives just the way they are. We don't need to change or fix anything about ourselves or others.

Living in the heart means finding this place of acceptance within. When we accept our lives the way they are, we rest in the truth of our being, which does not depend on what is happening outside of us. We rest in the realization that right here and right now we are worthy of love and so are others.

When we rest in the heart, we inhabit the present moment fully. We have a choice of what to think, how to feel, and when to act. We dwell at the place of power and possibility. We have the freedom to be ourselves completely.

When we rest in the heart, we do not act in compulsive ways. We do not act out our fear or indulge our desires. We recognize our fear and our desire and hold them with compassion. We sink down through the levels of emotional conflict or ambivalence to the place of acceptance. And there we stay until we know what we really want.

As we practice acceptance and dwell in the silence of our heart, what we really want becomes clear. The more we dwell in this place, the more our thoughts, feelings and actions become congruent. We become more honest, more authentic, more compassionate with ourselves and others.

Part Three

✤

The Surrendered Life

Expectations

We all have ideas of the way we want things to be. We expect certain results to come from our actions. We desire certain outcomes.

People often say "Don't have any expectations." But that is not realistic. We are going to have expectations, just as we are going to have judgments, fears and desires. It doesn't make sense to try to get rid of our expectations, just as it doesn't make sense to try to get rid of our judgments, our desires, and our fears. The real issue is "How do we hold our expectations when they come up?"

If we try to impose our expectations on the reality at hand, we will be disappointed if they are not met. If we pretend not to have expectations, we will be dishonest with ourselves and others.

Instead of imposing or denying our expectations, we just want to be aware of them and hold them with compassion. Then, we can accept the outcome regardless of whether our expectations are met.

Expectations arise in consciousness just as do fears, desires and judgments. We need to be aware of them and let them be. We don't need to hold onto them or try to push them away.

Life doesn't always show up the way we want it to. In fact, it could be said that the more we want it to show up a certain way, the less chance there is that it will happen that way. Our attachment to specific results often puts pressure on ourselves or others. It makes it more difficult for things to unfold naturally. As a result, we experience struggle and resistance.

The best results happen when we are clear about what we want, communicate well with others, and do the very best we can. Then, we can live without regret. Even if things show up differently from the way we expected them to, we don't take this personally. We don't feel that we have failed or that we are being punished.

Instead, we try to accept the situation as it is

and learn what we can from it. We don't stuff our disappointment and frustration, but acknowledge them, while keeping our hearts and minds open. We know that things can change, and what appeared to be a setback can sometimes become a blessing in disguise.

Life has its ups and downs, its ebb and its flow. The same variation can be found in our own consciousness. Sometimes we are joyful; other times we are sad. Sometimes we are confident and loving; other times we are fearful and defensive.

Consciousness is composed of waves of thought and feeling. External events have the same kind of fluctuation.

If you stop life at any moment and look at it, you will get a very narrow picture. It won't be accurate. You have to watch the waves come and go in order to see the whole picture. This requires patience.

When we are patient, we know that things are always changing. Peaks become valleys. Sadness yields to joy. What seems like failure might be success in disguise. Life is not always what it appears to be. We have to surrender what we know to discover what we don't know.

Staying in the Present

Regardless of what happened yesterday, last week or last year, we have a new situation with new choices available to us right now. The pain or frustration of the past does not have to become present pain or frustration. Even if the external situation seems the same as it did in the past, we can bring a new perspective to it.

The present always offers us a different perception or a different choice, if we are willing to see it. The question is "Are we willing?"

To be sure, it is easier to see the past than it is to see the present. The past does not change. We know what it looks like, so we don't have to be alert. Seeing the past lulls us to sleep. Being in the present requires our full, conscious attention.

If you want to see someone skilled in being in

the present, observe athletes in a basketball, foot-ball, or hockey game. The action is constantly changing. Every pick or block or check creates new possibilities. Seeing those possibilities as soon as they emerge is essential. If the athlete does not stay alert, s/he may lose the ball or the puck. The best players are not only those who have the greatest physical skills, but the ones who are most alert to the flow of the game and the action at hand.

If we are going to be successful in our lives, we need to cultivate our ability to be present and alert. We can develop a game plan that takes into account what has happened in the past, but when the action starts we need to be focused on the present. If the game plan isn't working, we need to revise it or drop it completely.

Having an open heart and open mind helps us stay alert in the moment. When we are alert, we bring patience, flexibility and willingness to each situation. We sink down through our judgments, our desires, and our fears to the essence of our being, where we can respond uniquely and appropriately to the situation at hand.

Learning from the Past

The best way to put the past behind us is to learn from it. When we make mistakes, we can see the consequences to ourselves and others. We can apologize and make amends to others. We can forgive ourselves and learn from our errors.

When we learn from our mistakes, we don't repeat them. The past stays past. It isn't carried forward.

When we find that we are constantly repeating past patterns, there is a good chance that we haven't learned from our mistakes. We may be focused on what other people did, blaming them for our misfortune, rather than looking at our own actions.

Until we are willing to take responsibility for our own actions, we aren't likely to learn from our mistakes. When we forgive others and begin looking at ourselves, we begin to tune into how we helped to create misunderstanding or misfortune. Understanding our part is essential, because that is the only part we can change. We can't change how others have acted or how they might act in the future.

Ironically, those who are constantly referencing the past — limiting their present choices by holding onto old wounds — are precisely those who have not acknowledged their mistakes or learned from them. They are attached to the past because they have not learned to take responsibility for it. And they will remain attached until they see their errors and atone for them.

It is important to see just how frequently we reference the past. On the one hand, we say that we want something different to happen in our lives; yet, on the other hand, we are still focused on what happened before. We keep bringing the past up in our conversations and using it as evidence for why we can't change.

The truth is, we must be willing to change or our life will continue as usual. We must be willing to see our mistakes and correct them if we want today to be different than yesterday.

If we are seeing the present moment through the lens of the past, we are very likely to create the past all over again. What we give our attention to tends to prosper.

Changes in our thinking can have immediate effect if we are confident in them. But that means that we stop talking about all the things that went wrong in the past.

The past is over. We are not the same person we were then. This is a new time, a new place, a new situation. But most important, our consciousness has changed. We've seen our mistakes and are determined to learn from them. In the past, we may have acted unconsciously, blindly, compulsively. Now, we are acting consciously, with freedom and intention.

We stop saying *I can't* because of what happened in the past and we start saying *I can* because I am a different person. I have learned from my errors.

We go from being disempowered by the past by to being empowered by it. As a victim of the past, I am condemned to repeat it. As a learner and a corrector of my mistakes, I am a creator of a new and different future.

Taking the Next Step

It's easy to get carried away planning our futures. But life is generally unkind to "The best made plans of mice and men." No matter how hard we try, the future cannot be predicted.

The best that we can do is to be clear about our goals and have a flexible strategy for reaching them. As the situation evolves, we may find that we have to revise our strategy several times.

We may know where we want to go, but we can't always control how we are going to get there. The "how" — the means we take to reach our goals — may have to be modified to deal with unanticipated obstacles that appear in our way. What is clear, however, is that if we are committed to our goal, we will eventually achieve it.

However, it may take longer than we anticipated. The route we take may be more circuitous than the one we had planned to take.

When it comes down to it, the most that we can know with certainty is what our next step is. In order to connect with that inner certainty, we often need to let go of our elaborate plans and just ask "What is the next step? What feels good to me right now?"

It may not satisfy our egos to know the next step — our egos often want to know everything right now — but knowing what's next can bring clarity to our minds and peace to our hearts. We know what to focus on. We know where to put our energies.

The more skillful we become in being present in the moment, the more we will realize that knowing the next step is enough. We don't need to know what's going to happen next week, or next month, or next year. We just need to know what feels right now.

Even if it were possible to know what is going

to happen in a month or a year's time, we would not necessarily benefit from that knowledge. Indeed, knowing the future might actually prevent us from doing things that we need to do right now. If we knew that a project would not succeed, we might not give it our best energy. And that might prevent us from accomplishing something that is key to helping us move in a new direction in the future.

Knowing what's next enables us to put our best energy into the present moment. As long as we keep doing that, our future takes care of itself.

When we become bogged down in mechanics of our future projects, we lose our clarity. We become preoccupied with "shoulds" and "what ifs." The result is confusion or frustration. Time and energy that could be invested in the present moment are squandered. We lose our focus, our faith and our optimism.

At such moments, we need to take a deep breath and bring our attention to the present. We need to ask ourselves "What can I do with energy and clarity right now?" That will ground us.

If the answer is "There is nothing to do right now," then we need to take a break or give our attention to something else. Often, when a new direction wants to emerge, we need to stop what we are doing and allow the new energy a chance to make itself known and felt.

In this sense, the pause between actions is as important as the actions themselves. It creates an opportunity for revision, reshaping, and redirection.

Periods of rest and relaxation are as important to the well being of our consciousness as are periods of activity. Rest supports activity. Activity necessitates rest.

One of the keys to living a life filled with grace is understanding when we need to rest and when we need to work. For there is an ideal time for each.

Ecclesiastes tell us "To everything there is a season, a time to reap and a time to sew, a time for every purpose under heaven." If we stay in the present moment and keep asking "What's the next step?" we will stay connected with the ebb and flow of life. We will work when it is time to work and rest when it is time to rest. We will be alone when it is time to be alone, and we will be with others when it is a time for sharing. We will move with the current of the river, instead of against it. We will cooperate with life, instead of opposing it. That is how our struggle is surrendered. That is how grace in born in our lives.

Part Four

❧

Grace Unfolding

Surrender Invites Grace

Now we are aware of our judgments, fears, desires, and expectations as they come up. We see how we resist life and push it away. And we have learned to hold all of this gently and with compassion.

We don't beat ourselves up for having fears or judgments or for making mistakes. We have learned to take a deep breath and sink down through all the contractions of consciousness to rest in the truth of our being.

Moment by moment, we find a way to accept and accommodate whatever life brings our way. Sometimes that might mean taking a step back. Sometimes it might mean taking a step forward.

We do the best we can with the understanding that we have at the time. Yet we know that life is our teacher and that we always have more to learn. When life brings us unexpected challenges, we use them to grow in understanding and compassion for ourselves and others.

This is the attitude of surrender that attracts grace into our lives. Grace flows naturally through an open mind and an open heart. When we give our lives over to the truth of our being, the abundance of the universe flows through our heads, our hearts, and our hands.

Saint Francis used to pray "Let me be thy instrument." As we surrender more and more deeply to the truth of our being, each one of us becomes a channel through which the divine presence flows. The clarity and wisdom of the divine express through our open minds. The love and compassion of the divine express through our open hearts. The grace and abundance of the divine flow through our surrendered lives.

Unity vs. Duality Consciousness

We are walking a tightrope between two very different perceptions of ourselves. One perception says that we are perfect as we are; we don't need to be fixed or changed in any way. The other perception says that we make mistakes and we need to learn from them to realize our full potential.

In the unity perception, improvement is not necessary. We are each perfect just as we are right now. In the dualistic perception, improvement and psychological growth are essential if we are to become ourselves more fully.

Unity perception says *I am God*. Duality perception says *I am becoming God*.

As long as I am holding the consciousness of my perfection and yours, there is nothing to fix. There is no such thing as a problem or a mistake. There is no fear, doubt, judgment or expectation here. There is no time or space. There is only God: eternity manifesting in this moment and in this place.

But as soon as I make a single judgment about you or about myself, as soon as fear comes up for me, or my expectations are not met, I find myself moving into dualistic perception. This is the psychological equivalent of the mythic fall from grace.

Now, it is my belief that something is wrong.

There is a problem. Someone needs to change. Something needs to be fixed. A mistake has been made and it needs to be corrected. I am no longer living in unity consciousness. I am living in dualistic consciousness. Here there is good and bad, high and low, success and failure. Here, judgment and comparison are a way of life. Some people are kinder or more moral than others. Here, we have crime, punishment, and even redemption.

In unity consciousness, there is no need for redemption because there is no fall from grace. There is no need for forgiveness because there is no sin, transgression or mistake.

Unity consciousness and duality consciousness are two different worlds. Each one of us lives in both worlds at various times in our experience. The distance between these worlds is the distance between one thought and another.

Judgment initiates the fall from grace. Forgiveness initiates the return to living in grace.

Forgiveness as a Way of Life

When judgment comes up, forgiveness is its antidote. When I judge you, I come back to grace by owning the judgment. I know it is about me, not about you. And I forgive myself for not feeling worthy and for projecting that unworthiness on you.

When you judge me, I realize that your judgment is about you, not about me. I feel compassion for you and I hope that you can see your self-judgment and forgive it, so that you too can return to grace.

If we make the judgment real, we fall further and further away from God consciousness. We move into blame and shame, attack and defense. Heaven becomes a living hell. The divine becomes human and is crucified on a tree.

The question is: who died on the tree? Is it a man or a God, or both at the same time?

The cross represents both our divinity and our humanity. Jesus was not the only one who carried a cross, nor will he be the only one to suffer and die upon it.

Each one of us moves between these two worlds. Some of us are descending to earth. Some of us are rising to heaven. We have all taken the journey both ways. We know this rollercoaster. The wheel of Karma turns, and we turn with it.

Only when it occurs to us that we might be able to lay down our cross and get off the wheel of karma, do we step out on the spiritual path. Only then do we become earnest enough to practice.

What then is the practice?

It is very simple. To stay in God consciousness, do not judge. Do not entertain doubts or fears. Do not be attached to the past or have expectations of the future. If you can do this, then you already sitting with Jesus and Buddha.

If you can't do this, or if you can do it only for moments at a time, then you need to practice forgiveness. You need to bring a loving/unity consciousness into your experience of duality.

How do you do this? You start by acknowledging your mistake. You accept it and take responsibility for it. You don't try to blame anyone else.

Instead of beating yourself up, you try to be gentle with yourself. You realize that the only way you can put your mistake behind you is to learn from it. You get in touch with the fear which provoked your thought or action. You stay with the fear until you can move through it. You do your own healing.

Then you make amends to others you have hurt. You ask for their understanding. You make restitution. And you forgive yourself. You release the past, knowing that you will make a different choice in the future.

Every time you make a judgment, some version of the forgiveness process is necessary. You can't learn to forgive if you don't practice. Every day you have hundreds of opportunities to own your mistakes and forgive them.

Forgiveness enables us to move out of duality into unity consciousness. When we have forgiven and atoned for our mistakes, we are no longer guilty. Our innocence is restored. Our consciousness has shifted. We are not the same person who made the mistake.

Forgiveness helps me to return to grace, to remember that I am perfect the way I am and that you are perfect the way you are. It helps me remember that neither one of us needs to be fixed. Life is totally acceptable the way it is. I don't have to resist it or try to change it. I can flow with reality as it unfolds.

I surrender my ego consciousness by accepting it the way it is. I don't try to get rid of it. I don't let it take charge of my life. I just acknowledge that it is there. I become aware of the ups and downs within my consciousness just as I am aware of the ups and downs in my external life. I ride the waves of consciousness and experience, holding it all in compassionate awareness.

My judgments, my fears, my expectations rest now in something larger, wider and deeper than the egoic consciousness that gives them birth. They rest in my loving acceptance. They rest in my awareness that whatever is happening right now in this moment is perfect. It is exactly as it needs to be.

In each moment that we live, we move in and out of divine consciousness. We fall from grace and ascend to the altar of forgiveness. We make mistakes and atone for them. We make judgments, own them, and forgive ourselves. We practice being the presence of God and the one who forgets our divine origin.

That is the nature of our journey. It is not linear, but cyclical. What we can't forgive now, comes around again and again for our attention.

We seem to move toward the goal of self-realization, yet that goal can only be realized to the extent that we love and accept ourselves here and now. In that sense, we have reached the goal many times.

We have remembered and forgotten. We have awakened and fallen back to sleep. But all this means nothing, because no matter what we have done or will do, we only have this time and this place.

If love isn't happening right now, it isn't happening. It doesn't matter how many Buddhas or Christs have come before us or will come after us.

For years we have prayed to the Divine thinking that It was apart from us. Let us pray together now, knowing that the Divine Heart is not separate from our heart, nor the Divine Mind separate from our mind.

A Prayer

Father and Mother of All that I AM, may I be fully present in this time and this place. May I accept myself just the way I am. May I accept my brothers and sisters just the way they are. May I accept life as it is unfolding right now.

Make I take All that Is into my heart and be at peace with it. May All that Is be at peace with me. May I give and receive that blessing. May I dwell in that communion.

May I surrender my little will to your great Will which holds all beings in perfect equality. May I surrender the conditions I place on love that I may give love and receive love without conditions.

May my heart open, releasing fear and desire. May my mind open, releasing judgments and interpretations. May my life open, releasing expectations, so that I may embrace what is and see it truly.

May my openness invite your presence. May my surrender inspire your grace.

Amen.

Paul Ferrini is the author of numerous books which help us heal the emotional body and embrace a spirituality grounded in the real challenges of daily life. Paul's work is heart-centered and experiential, empowering us to move through our fear and shame and share who we are authentically with others. Paul Ferrini founded and edited Miracles Magazine, a publication devoted to telling Miracle Stories offering hope and inspiration to all of us. Paul's conferences, retreats and Affinity Group Process have helped thousands of people deepen their practice of forgiveness and open their hearts to the Divine presence in themselves and others. For more information on Paul's workshops and retreats or The Affinity Group Process, contact Heartways Press, P.O. Box 181, South Deerfield, MA 01373 or call 413-665-0555.

New Titles from Heartways Press

Part IV of the Reflections of the Christ Mind Series is Hot off the Press

Return to the Garden
Reflections of The Christ Mind,
Part IV
$12.95, Paperback
ISBN # 1-879159-35-X

"In the beginning, we lived in blind obedience to the law. We did what we were told and we were rewarded appropriately. All our needs were provided for. We knew no struggle or hardship. We were God's beloved. But happiness was not enough for us. We wanted the freedom to live our own lives. Like Prometheus, we had to steel the fire of the gods. We had no choice. To evolve, we had to learn to become love-givers, not just love-receivers.

We all know what happened then. We were cast out of the Garden and for the first time in our lives we felt shame, jealousy, anger, lack. We experienced highs and lows, joy and sorrow, summer and winter. As we descended into the world of duality, our lives became difficult. We had to work hard to survive. We had to make mistakes and learn from them.

Initially, we tried to blame others for our mistakes. But that did not make our lives any easier. It just deepened our pain and misery. We moved from the Garden of Eden to the Garden of Golgotha. The fall from grace continued throughout endless cycles of attack and defense, until I was crucified on a cross. That was the turning point. Not just for me, but for all of us. From that point onward, we had to learn to take others off the hook and become responsible for our own mistakes. The time for blaming others was over.

From that moment, we had to learn to hold our neighbor's good equally with our own, to face our fears, instead of projecting them onto each other. We had to learn to become responsible for all our thoughts, feelings and experiences. Not only were we asked to learn the Truth, we were asked to internalize It, to become It.

This mythic journey has taken us from unconscious innocence to conscious experience, from selfish actions to the awareness of our mistakes, from guilt to self-forgiveness. Gradually, we have learned to take responsibility for our creations and to hold our fears and judgments with compassion.

Returning to the Garden, we are different from the way we were when we left. We left hellbent on expressing our creativity at any cost. We return humble and sensitive to the needs of all. We return not just as created, but as Creator, not just as son of man, but son of God. From Adam to Christ, we come full circle."

Learn the Spiritual Practice
Associated with the Christ Mind Teachings

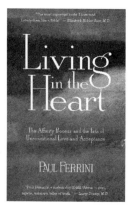

Living in the Heart
The Affinity Process
and the Path of
Unconditional Love
and Acceptance
Paperback $10.95
ISBN 1-879159-36-8

The long awaited, definitive book on the *Affinity Process* is finally here. For years, the *Affinity Process* has been refined by participants so that it could be easily understood and experienced. Now, you can learn how to hold a safe, loving, non-judgmental space for yourself and others which will enable you to open your heart and move through your fears. The *Affinity Process* will help you learn to take responsibility for your fears and judgments so that you won't project them onto others. It will help you learn to listen deeply and without judgment to others. And it will teach you how to tell your truth clearly without blaming others for your experience.

Part One contains an in-depth description of the principles on which the *Affinity Process* is based. Part Two contains a detailed discussion of the *Affinity Group* Guidelines. And Part Three contains a manual for people who wish to facilitate an *Affinity Group* in their community.

If you are a serious student of the Christ Mind teachings, this book is essential for you. It will enable you to begin a spiritual practice which will transform your life and the lives of others. It will also offer you a way of extending the teachings of love and forgiveness throughout your community.

Now Finally our Bestselling Title on Audio Tape

Love Without Conditions, Reflections
of the Christ Mind, Part I
by Paul Ferrini

The Book on Tape
Read by the Author
2 Cassettes,
Approximately 3.25 hours

ISBN 1-879159-24-4 $19.95

Now on audio tape: the incredible book from Jesus calling us to awaken to our own Christhood. Listen to this gentle, profound book while driving in your car or before going to sleep at night. Elisabeth Kubler-Ross calls this "The most important book I have read. I study it like a Bible." Find out for yourself how this amazing book has helped thousands of people understand the radical teachings of the master and begin to integrate these teachings into their lives.

Heartways Press

"Integrating Spirituality into Daily Life"
More Books by Paul Ferrini

With its heartfelt combination of sensuality and spirituality, Paul Ferrini's poetry has been compared to the poetry of Rumi.

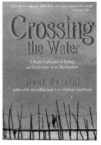

• Crossing The Water
Poems About Healing and Forgiveness in Our Relationships

The time for healing and reconciliation has come, Ferrini writes. Our relationships help us heal childhood wounds, walk through our deepest fears, and cross over the water of our emotional pain. Just as the rocks in the river are *pounded and caressed to rounded stone,* the rough edges of our personalities are worn smooth in the context of a committed relationship. If we can keep our hearts open, we can heal together, experience genuine equality, and discover what it means to give and receive love without conditions.

With its heartfelt combination of sensuality and spirituality, Paul Ferrini's poetry has been compared to the poetry of Rumi. These luminous poems demonstrate why Paul Ferrini is first a poet, a lover and a mystic. Come to this feast of the beloved with an open heart and open ears. 96 pp. paper ISBN 1-879159-25-2 $9.95.

• Miracle of Love, Reflections of the Christ Mind, Part III

Many people say that this latest volume of the Christ Mind series is the best yet. Jesus tells us "I was born to a simple woman in a barn. She was no more a virgin than your mother was." Moreover, he tells us, the virgin birth is not the only myth surrounding his life and teaching. So are the concepts of vicarious atonement and physical resurrection.

Relentlessly, the master tears down the rigid dogma and hierarchical teachings that obscure his simple message of love and forgiveness. He encourages us to take him down from the pedestal and the cross and see him as an equal brother who found the way out of suffering by opening his heart totally. We too can open our hearts and find peace and happiness. "The power of love will make miracles in your life as wonderful as any attributed to me," he tells us. "Your birth into this embodiment is no less holy than mine. The love that you extend to others is no less important than the love I extend to you." 192 pp. paper ISBN 1-879159-23-6 $12.95.

• Waking Up Together Illuminations on the Road to Nowhere

There comes a time for all of us when the outer destinations no longer satisfy and we finally understand that the love and happiness we seek cannot be found outside of us. It must be found in our own hearts, on the other side of our pain. "The Road to Nowhere is the path through your heart. It is not a journey of escape. It is a journey through your pain to end the pain of separation."

This book makes it clear that we can no longer rely on outer teachers or teachings to find our spiritual identity. Nor can we find who we are in relationships where boundaries are blurred and one person makes decisions for another. If we want to be authentic, we can't allow anyone else to be an authority for us, nor can we allow ourselves to be an authority for another person.

Authentic relationships happen between equal partners who take responsibility for their own consciousness and experience. When their buttons are pushed, they are willing to look at the obstacles they have erected to the experience of love and acceptance. As they understand and surrender the false ideas and emotional reactions that create separation, genuine intimacy becomes possible, and the sacred dimension of the relationship is born. 216 pp. paper ISBN 1-879159-17-1 $14.95

• **The Ecstatic Moment:**
A Practical Manual for Opening Your Heart and Staying in It.

A simple, power-packed guide that helps us take appropriate responsibility for our experience and establish healthy boundaries with others. Part II contains many helpful exercises and meditations that teach us to stay centered, clear and open in heart and mind. The Affinity Group Process and other group practices help us learn important listening and communication skills that can transform our troubled relationships. Once you have read this book, you will keep it in your briefcase or on your bedside table, referring to it often. You will not find a more practical, down to earth guide to contemporary spirituality. You will want to order copies for all your friends. 128 pp. paper ISBN 1-879159-18-X $10.95

• **The Silence of the Heart**
Reflections of the Christ Mind,
Part II

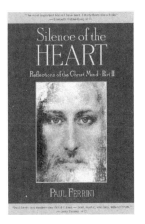

A powerful sequel to *Love Without Conditions*. John Bradshaw says "With deep insight and sparkling clarity, this book demonstrates that the roots of all abuse are to be found in our own self-betrayal. Paul Ferrini leads us skillfully and courageously beyond shame, blame, and attachment to our wounds into the depths of self-forgiveness. It is a must-read for all people who are ready to take responsibility for their own healing." 218 pp. paper. ISBN 1-879159-16-3 $14.95

• Love Without Conditions:
Reflections of the Christ Mind, Part I
An incredible book from Jesus calling us to awaken to our Christhood. Rarely has any book conveyed the teachings of the master in such a simple but profound manner. This book will help you to bring your understanding from the head to the heart so that you can model the teachings of love and forgiveness in your daily life. 192 pp. paper ISBN 1-879159-15-15 $12.00

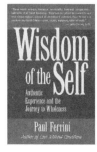

• The Wisdom of the Self
This ground-breaking book explores our authentic experience and our journey to wholeness. "Your life is your spiritual path. Don't be quick to abandon it for promises of bigger and better experiences. You are getting exactly the experiences you need to grow. If your growth seems too slow or uneventful for you, it is because you have not fully embraced the situations and relationships at hand. To know the Self is to allow everything, to embrace the totality of who we are, all that we think and feel, all of our fear, all of our love." 229 pp. paper ISBN 1-879159-14-7 $12.00

• The Twelve Steps of Forgiveness
A practical manual for healing ourselves and our relationships. This book gives us a step-by-step process for moving through our fears, projections, judgments, and guilt so that we can take responsibility for creating the life we want. With great gentleness, we learn to embrace our lessons and to find equality with others. A must read for all in recovery and others seeking spiritual wholeness. 128 pp. paper ISBN 1-879159-10-4 $10.00

• **The Wounded Child's Journey**
Into Love's Embrace

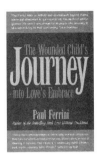

This book explores a healing process in which we confront our deep-seated guilt and fear, bringing love and forgiveness to the wounded child within. By surrendering our judgments of self and others, we overcome feelings of separation and dismantle co-dependent patterns that restrict our self-expression and ability to give and receive love. 225pp. paper ISBN 1-879159-06-6 $12.00

• **The Bridge to Reality**

A Heart-Centered Approach to *A Course in Miracles* and the Process of Inner Healing. Sharing his experiences of spiritual awakening, Paul emphasizes self-acceptance and forgiveness as cornerstones of spiritual practice. Presented with beautiful photos, this book conveys the essence of *The Course* as it is lived in daily life. 192 pp. paper ISBN 1-879159-03-1 $12.00

• **From Ego to Self**

108 illustrated affirmations designed to offer you a new way of viewing conflict situations so that you can overcome negative thinking and bring more energy, faith and optimism into your life. 144 pp. paper ISBN 1-879159-01-5 $10.00

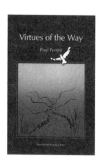

• **Virtues of The Way**

A lyrical work of contemporary scripture reminiscent of the Tao Te Ching. Beautifully illustrated, this inspirational book will help you cultivate the spiritual values required to fulfill your creative purpose and live in harmony with others. 64 pp. paper ISBN 1-879159-02-3 $7.50

• **The Body of Truth**

A crystal clear introduction to the universal teachings of love and forgiveness. This book traces all forms of suffering to negative attitudes and false beliefs, which we have the ability to transform. 64 pp. paper ISBN 1-879159-02-3 $7.50

• **Available Light**

Inspirational, passionate poems dealing with the work of inner integration, love and relationships, death and re-birth, loss and abundance, life purpose and the reality of spiritual vision. 128 pp. paper ISBN 1-879159-05-8 $12.00

Poetry and Guided Meditation Tapes
by Paul Ferrini

The Poetry of the Soul

With its heartfelt combination of sensuality and spirituality, Paul Ferrini's poetry has been compared to the poetry of Rumi. These luminous poems demonstrate why Paul Ferrini is first a poet, a lover and a mystic. Come to this feast of the beloved with an open heart and open ears. With Suzi Kesler on piano. $10.00 ISBN 1-879159-26-0

The Circle of Healing

The meditation and healing tape that many of you have been seeking. This gentle meditation opens the heart to love's presence and extends that love to all the beings in your experience. A powerful tape with inspirational piano accompaniment by Michael Gray. ISBN 1-879159-08-2 $10.00

Healing the Wounded Child

A potent healing tape that accesses old feelings of pain, fragmentation, self-judgment and separation and brings them into the light of conscious awareness and acceptance. Side two includes a hauntingly beautiful "inner child" reading from *The Bridge to Reality* with piano accompaniment by Michael Gray. ISBN 1-879159-11-2 $10.00

Forgiveness: Returning to the Original Blessing

A self healing tape that helps us accept and learn from the mistakes we have made in the past. By letting go of our judgments and ending our ego-based search for perfection, we can bring our darkness to the light, dissolving anger, guilt, and shame. Piano accompaniment by Michael Gray. ISBN 1-879159-12-0 $10.00

Paul Ferrini Talks and Workshop Tapes

Answering Our Own Call for Love *A Sermon given at the Pacific Church of Religious Science in San Diego, CA November, 1997*

Paul tells the story of his own spiritual awakening, his Atheist upbringing, and how he began to open to the presence of God and his connection with Jesus and the Christ Mind teaching. In a very clear, heartfelt way, Paul presents to us the spiritual path of love, acceptance, and forgiveness. Also available on videotape. 1 Cassette *$10.00 ISBN 1-879159-33-3*

The Ecstatic Moment *A workshop given by Paul in Los Angeles at the Agape International Center of Truth, May, 1997*

Shows us how we can be with our pain compassionately and learn to nurture the light within ourselves, even when it appears that we are walking through darkness. Discusses subjects such as living in the present, acceptance, not fixing self or others, being with our discomfort and learning that we are lovable as we are. *1 Cassette $10.00 ISBN 1-879159-27-9*

Honoring Self and Other *A Workshop at the Pacific Church of Religious Science in San Diego, November, 1997*

Helps us understand the importance of not betraying ourselves in our relationships with others. Focuses on understanding healthy boundaries, setting limits, and saying no to others in a loving way. Real life examples include a woman who is married to a man who is chronically critical of her, and a gay man who wants to tell his judgmental parents that he has AIDS. *1 Cassette $10.00 ISBN 1-879159-34-1*

Seek First the Kingdom *Two Sunday Messages given by Paul: the first in May, 1997 in Los Angeles at the Agape Int'l. Center of Truth, and the second in September, 1997 in Portland, OR at the Unity Church.*

Discusses the words of Jesus in the Sermon on the Mount: "Seek first the kingdom and all else will be added to you." Helps us understand how we create the inner temple by learning to hold our judgments of self and other more compassionately. The love of God flows through our love and acceptance of ourselves. As we establish our connection to the divine within ourselves, we don't need to look outside of ourselves for love and acceptance. Includes fabulous music by The Agape Choir and Band. *1 Cassette $10.00 ISBN 1-879159-30-9*

Double Cassette Tape Sets

Ending the Betrayal of the Self *A Workshop given by Paul at the Learning Annex in Toronto, April, 1997*

A roadmap for integrating the opposing voices in our psyche so that we can experience our own wholeness. Delineates what our responsibility is and isn't in our relationships with others, and helps us learn to set clear, firm, but loving boundaries. Our relationships can become areas of sharing and fulfillment, rather than mutual invitations to co-dependency and self betrayal. *2 Cassettes $16.95 ISBN 1-879159-28-7*

Relationships: Changing Past Patterns *A Talk with Questions and Answers Given at the Redondo Beach Church of Religious Science, 11/97*

Begins with a Christ Mind talk describing the link between learning to love and accept ourselves and learning to love and accept others. Helps us understand how we are invested in the past and continue to replay our old relationship stories. Helps us get clear on what we want and understand how to be faithful to it. By being totally committed to ourselves, we give birth to the beloved within and also without. Includes an in-depth discussion about meditation, awareness, hearing our inner voice, and the Affinity Group Process. *2 Cassettes $16.95 ISBN 1-879159-32-5*

Relationship As a Spiritual Path *A workshop given by Paul in Los Angeles at the Agape Int'l. Center of Truth, May, 1997*

Explores concrete ways in which we can develop a relationship with ourselves and learn to take responsibility for our own experience, instead of blaming others for our perceived unworthiness. Also discussed: accepting our differences, the new paradigm of relationship, the myth of the perfect partner, telling our truth, compassion vs. rescuing, the unavailable partner, abandonment issues, negotiating needs, when to say no, when to stay and work on a relationship and when to leave. *2 Cassettes $16.95 ISBN 1-879159-29-5*

Opening to Christ Consciousness *A Talk with Questions & Answers at Unity Church, Tustin, CA November, 1997*

Begins with a Christ Mind talk giving us a clear picture of how the divine spark dwells within each of us and how we can open up to God-consciousness on a regular basis. Deals with letting go and forgiveness in our relationships with our parents, our children and our partners. A joyful, funny, and scintillating tape you will want to listen to many times. Also available on videotape. *2 Cassettes $16.95 ISBN 1-879159-31-7*

Risen Christ Posters and Notecards

11"x17" Poster
suitable for framing
ISBN 1-879159-19-8 $10.00

Set of 8 Notecards
with Envelopes
ISBN 1-879159-20-1 $10.00

Ecstatic Moment Posters and Notecards

8.5"x11" Poster
suitable for framing
ISBN 1-879159-21-X $5.00

Set of 8 Notecards
with Envelopes
ISBN 1-879159-22-8 $10.00

Heartways Press Order Form

Name_____

Address_____

City _____State _____Zip _____

Phone _____

BOOKS BY PAUL FERRINI

Grace Unfolding ($9.95)   _____
Return to the Garden ($12.95)   _____
Living in the Heart ($10.95)   _____
Miracle of Love ($12.95)   _____
Crossing the Water ($9.95)   _____
Waking Up Together ($14.95)   _____
The Ecstatic Moment ($10.95)   _____
The Silence of the Heart ($14.95)   _____
Love Without Conditions ($12.00)   _____
The Wisdom of the Self ($12.00)   _____
The Twelve Steps of Forgiveness ($10.00)   _____
The Circle of Atonement ($12.00)   _____
The Bridge to Reality ($12.00)   _____
From Ego to Self ($10.00)   _____
Virtues of the Way ($7.50)   _____
The Body of Truth ($7.50)   _____
Available Light ($10.00)   _____

AUDIO TAPES BY PAUL FERRINI

The Circle of Healing ($10.00)   _____
Healing the Wounded Child ($10.00)   _____
Forgiveness: Returning to the Original Blessing ($10.00)   _____
The Poetry of the Soul ($10.00)   _____
Seek First the Kingdom ($10.00)   _____
Answering Our Own Call for Love ($10.00)   _____
The Ecstatic Moment ($10.00)   _____
Honoring Self and Other ($10.00)   _____
Love Without Conditions ($19.95) 2 tapes   _____
Ending the Betrayal of the Self ($16.95) 2 tapes   _____
Relationships: Changing Past Patterns ($16.95) 2 tapes   _____
Relationship As a Spiritual Path ($16.95) 2 tapes   _____
Opening to Christ Consciousness ($16.95) 2 tapes   _____

Continued on Backside

POSTERS AND NOTECARDS

Risen Christ Poster 11"x17" ($10.00)

Ecstatic Moment Poster 8.5"x11" ($5.00) _____

Risen Christ Notecards with envelopes 8/pkg ($10.00) _____

Ecstatic Moment Notecards with envelopes 8/pkg ($10.00) _____

SHIPPING

($2.00 for first item, $1.00 each additional item.
Add additional $1.00 for first class postage.)
MA residents please add 5% sales tax. _____

TOTAL $ _____

Please allow 1-2 weeks for delivery

Send Order To: Heartways Press
P. O. Box 181, South Deerfield, MA 01373
413-665-0555 • 413-665-4565 (fax)
Toll free: 1-888-HARTWAY (Orders only)

Heartways Press Order Form

Name_____

Address_____

City _____State _____Zip _____

Phone _____

BOOKS BY PAUL FERRINI

Grace Unfolding ($9.95)   _____

Return to the Garden ($12.95)   _____

Living in the Heart ($10.95)   _____

Miracle of Love ($12.95)   _____

Crossing the Water ($9.95)   _____

Waking Up Together ($14.95)   _____

The Ecstatic Moment ($10.95)   _____

The Silence of the Heart ($14.95)   _____

Love Without Conditions ($12.00)   _____

The Wisdom of the Self ($12.00)   _____

The Twelve Steps of Forgiveness ($10.00) _____

The Circle of Atonement ($12.00)   _____

The Bridge to Reality ($12.00)   _____

From Ego to Self ($10.00)   _____

Virtues of the Way ($7.50)   _____

The Body of Truth ($7.50)   _____

Available Light ($10.00)   _____

AUDIO TAPES BY PAUL FERRINI

The Circle of Healing ($10.00)   _____

Healing the Wounded Child ($10.00) _____

Forgiveness: Returning to the Original Blessing ($10.00) _____

The Poetry of the Soul ($10.00)   _____

Seek First the Kingdom ($10.00)   _____

Answering Our Own Call for Love ($10.00) _____

The Ecstatic Moment ($10.00)   _____

Honoring Self and Other ($10.00)   _____

Love Without Conditions ($19.95) 2 tapes _____

Ending the Betrayal of the Self ($16.95) 2 tapes _____

Relationships: Changing Past Patterns ($16.95) 2 tapes _____

Relationship As a Spiritual Path ($16.95) 2 tapes _____

Opening to Christ Consciousness ($16.95) 2 tapes _____

Continued on Backside

POSTERS AND NOTECARDS
Risen Christ Poster 11"x17" ($10.00)   _____
Ecstatic Moment Poster 8.5"x11" ($5.00)   _____
Risen Christ Notecards with envelopes 8/pkg ($10.00)   _____
Ecstatic Moment Notecards with envelopes 8/pkg ($10.00)   _____

SHIPPING
($2.00 for first item, $1.00 each additional item.
Add additional $1.00 for first class postage.)   _____
MA residents please add 5% sales tax.   _____

                                        TOTAL $ _____

Please allow 1-2 weeks for delivery

Send Order To: Heartways Press
P. O. Box 181, South Deerfield, MA 01373
413-665-0555 • 413-665-4565 (fax)
Toll free: 1-888-HARTWAY (Orders only)